COAT THIEF

Saint Julian Press

Poetry

Praise for *Coat Thief*

"Like walking meditations, the poetic feet of Jeffrey Davis's *Coat Thief* invoke mindfulness through grounded, regular movement. Profoundly attuned to the beauty of daily existence, these poems upend and expand conventional perceptions of magnitude as they give prominence to sneaker prints, earthworms, egg cartons, and other often unnoticed objects. These are poems filled with wonder, poems that demonstrate over and over that we need not rely on esoteric experience for transcendence—because it is, we learn from *Coat Thief,* the ordinary that is most extraordinary. Yes! It is possible for poetic feet to connect our soles and souls more intimately to the earth, and with Davis, the closer we are to the earth, the closer we are to the divine."

~ Melissa Studdard, *I Ate The Cosmos for Breakfast*

"The quiet moments of a life can be the most revealing and yet the ones we pay attention to least. Jeffrey Davis slows down the mind-camera in *Coat Thief* to linger in those moments with a focus always rich with compassion, empathy, and physical touch. I love his intention. I love his sound."

~ Kazim Ali, *Sky Ward*

"We are accustomed to poems that seek political change by deploying fierce urgency and by speeding up time to get us moving toward progress. But if the poems in Jeffrey Davis's *Coat Thief* are good evidence, then the most effective, and affective, poems of change may be those poems that slow time down and bless us with moments in which we are able to perceive emotional complexes in instants of time, moments that leave us "stupendously awake in the dark": an earthworm churning through the detritus of civilizations; wasting your morning speaking to a blue stone that is just beginning to hear you; a mother and the child kicking inside her with a god's foot."

~ Brian Clements, author of *Disappointed Psalms* and
   A Book of Common Rituals

COAT THIEF

Poems

By

Jeffrey Davis

Saint Julian Press
Houston

Published by
SAINT JULIAN PRESS, Inc.
2053 Cortlandt, Suite 200
Houston, Texas 77008

www.saintjulianpress.com

ISBN-13: 978-0-9965231-3-4
ISBN: 0-9965231-3-8
Library of Congress Control Number: 2016930829

Cover Art
Mark Rothko's *Untitled - [Blue, Green, and Brown]* 1952
All works by Rothko © 1998 Kate Rothko Prizel and Christopher Rothko
Artists Rights Society (ARS), New York

Author's Photo Credit: Franco Vogt

CONTENTS

1

2

3

4

[E]ach day is a god, and holiness holds forth in time.
- Annie Dillard

COAT THIEF

1

A Promise

I roll over. Your mother, wide awake at 2 am,
secures my palm on her warm belly mound.

Comfort, she needs comfort, reassurance
I love her, that we will weather this disaster,

that a burning house and becoming pregnant
in the same year may be an odd blessing,

and as my words try to break sleep's fog,
my palm feels what has awakened her–

you for the first time also rolling over,
a humpback whale raising its hello.

Melon motion teasing your papa's palm,
are you knocking? What can I tell you?

Sprout, it gets dark out here too, and cold
and, if you pay attention, strange.

You roll over. Yes, a god's foot brushes my palm,
a trout stealing breath that flips and vanishes.

Darkness, My Wise Little Brother

When darkness appears
outside your kitchen window
this winter bring him in
offer him a chipped cup of tea
and bring him so close
you can feel beneath
his thick coat
that hidden sorrow
known well by the nightingale
the gray wolf and other creatures
intimate with the skin of night

Hold him,
and he will tell you stories
of blind men's dreams and groundhogs' beds
of forgotten soldiers' songs
and the quiet wind that sneaks
through widows' doors
and then he will without shame
beg to ride your back into light

When you've fallen asleep
beside the dreaming fire
he will slip out the back,
the redolent scent of spring left
in his sneaker prints

Where Our Feet Take Us

When I finish raking, my great-grandmother calls me
indoors and lets me rub her feet with lotion. She lies on the
bed, watching *Days of Our Lives* pass by, her dyed brown hair
slightly blown by the blue metal fan. My small hands, red
from raking and rubbing, work her knobby feet, the
bobbing bunions passed down that bend my toes outward
as if I fell twenty feet and landed on my big toes' insides.
Purple veins run above her feet, aqueducts dousing arid
crops. Her flat dry feet wet with white rain, the toes
squirming desert worms, feet I never saw

when they wore rhinestone studded cowboy boots that
scuffed dusty saloon floors to the bars of Yellow Rose of
Texas. Her eyes that skirted the hundred carnival shows she
called "Show Bidness" and a thousand poker tables across
the Southwest where she and her lover latched diamonds
and furs and a Cadillac convertible, the pupils of a line of
pioneer women trying to hold on to something wild while
cities threatened to hold their souls indoors never budge
from the tube, though,

and I am not sure she feels the lotion until I think I hear the
fan moan but it's she who groans when I rub deep between
her toes where the skin cracks like mud and I fear the lotion
might sting but it seems to soothe instead like medicine or
memory when - her eyes at last closed - her lips that have
nursed a hundred pints of whiskey and a thousand packs of
Marlboros slowly break into a knowing grin and hum a
distant tune.

Gypsy Wife's Lament

From an airport corner I rattle
my tambourine, brass bones
that keep me from going home

Five months roaming Thailand's cryptic alleys
three months basking in torrid smells
of Greek fishers' mornings pregnant
with discreet possibility
Prague dusk promising a lyrical night
my hips awakened to the beats
of African drums and star-fire midnights
my breasts hung heavy
with the milk of sharing

On the ocean's other side,
where the plane waits to take me
well-defined rooms await.
Kitchen. Bedroom. Nursery. Office.
He will try to define my hours
and days will become picture framed again
by walls and errands, clients and cries.

Where does freedom fly?

My tambourine tempo clamors to find the music
in wallpapered voices, in hands soiled
by the same garden sowed and seeded
season after season, in the rhythms
of oatmeal and morning phone calls,
of seducing just that one man.

The rattle terrorizes gawkers who drop
rupees at my feet and dash away
a security guard is on his way
to silence me in his foreign tongue

but I must admit I am the foreigner
who struggles each day to find home
who suffers cat-calls when she walks alone
who seeks in Himalayan villages and exotic
rhythms her other faces.

A dervish twirl before the guard, I belt
a tune wandering with wonder
among familiar faces who know
my shadows' contours
who still will wake up
wrapped in me morning after
morning and call me exquisite
names like "maa" or "babe" ~
of drifting after twelve years of quilted
nights into forgotten valleys of that one
male body

bursting now at the top of my lungs
passengers clapping their hands

Coming home, coming home,
I'm coming home tonight.
Coming home, coming home,
I'm coming home tonight.

Coat Thief

I've been collecting coats along the streets for weeks in case
I'm caught naked this winter. Panic strikes me some nights
that I will awaken with nothing so I'm preparing.

Neighbors have surrendered their raggedy London Fogs,
their vinyl yellow rain slickers, even an old fox skin coat
with holes at the seams from someone's grandmother's
attic. Coats pile the back bedroom and cover my backyard
bushes like provisions.

I will not be caught naked this winter.

Go ahead, you say, and try to armor yourself with other
people's sleeves, but there's no getting ready for waking up
bewildered in the middle of the night in the middle of your
life in the middle of a downtown street with nothing, not
even your wits or your self, in your possession.

You could be walking down Lovers Lane, your briefcase in
hand, your heart in the other, and an SUV military vehicle
could whip by and strip you of your suit, your title, your
spouse, your house. You could be hiking after dark in
Montana's cryptic mountains, and lightning could strip you
of your boots, your roots, your backpack, your spine.

You could be stripped of everything at any moment.

So why wait, you say? Why not go naked, now? Live with
the lyric and let me sing you into a lyrical life, your body a
lyre whose strings strum along the beats of my heart's
drum.

Before I can respond, you strip me of all words and steal all
my coats.

Spring Break

The pond is cracking
a fissure down an icy body

A village chief shows a biologist
how to fish with the moon

The pond is cracking
a fissure down an icy mind

Rebels in Liberia refuse
to trade logs for lives

The pond is cracking
a beat into an icy heart

You can hear its drum
among ringing stillness

Roots are rising with questions.
What should you do?

Should you let yourself crack
and let the foundations fall
into the river banks?

A million maples' bodies pocked
with buds scream Yes,
the shoot ripping from your gut
lets you stay silent indoors no more.

The world awaits your arrival
waits to see your spring break
wide open and to become today uncontainable.

Earthworm, *Lumbricus Terrestris*

"It may be doubted whether there are many other creatures which have played so important a part in the history of the world." –Charles Darwin, 1881

Morning vermicelli for that big-bellied Robin,
angler's treasure to hook the big catch,
what do you feed on?
Soul food seeker,
you eat as you go,
the leafy debris of your path
feeding your fingery vermilion body,
your setae writhing
you to the beat of earth's drum,
earth's strum along your
cellular ear.

Who among us knows earth like you,
soil lover, your blood wine hue
so deep no wonder your moist body
feels its mate in earth's wet
innards, you who move
with a blind knowing into the underworld.

Earth's rap musician, body churning
to the cycles of city and soil,
you find the music and the food
in world's waste, soulful composter,
and break it down, break it down,
break it down.

Leveler of crops and civilizations,
humbler of earth's purported rulers,
you bring us to our knees
like children that we may see
you and see how small are we.

Stairwell

You have hammered your days to build
according to someone else's plans,
but nothing fits anymore.

Now you wonder how many nights
it takes to finish a stairwell
that ends at an unfinished room.

Resolve yourself instead to find a birch
alone in a meadow, its dried out limbs
fallen for the taking.

From the limbs whittle an armrest
whose contours match your desire.
Then carve the rest.

Compose the pieces the way
your hands and heart beat
to a lento patience–

no rush–

until the tree's limbs emerge as your seat,
a firm one suited only for your hips,
where you can rest and observe how many days

your friends plane away on wooden dreams
better used for kindling.

Maybe, one night, when the ashen sky
has cooled to the color of coal,
you will fit the leftover wood

into a series of steps in this room's corner
that will not take you very high,
but far enough to see from another perspective

your self reposed.

2

Today is the Day

This is the day
you were supposed to
be accountable

The eggs begged to be gathered
the beans to be counted
the books to be balanced

but you awoke instead
to your neighbor's peacock
strutting its song from the shed top

So you have wasted
the entire morning
speaking to blue stones

no, to just this one blue stone
that sits amidst a stream
its face like a grandmother
its weighty voice
you've just begun to hear

This is the day
you were supposed to be
accountable

What happened?

The sun slips past noon
and the peacock takes a nap
and all you can account for

is this one song you've made
for this one stone
who is just beginning to hear you

Climate Change

A rumbling under the bus seat to the city
jockeys the textures of missing you

the break of two wood ducks' necks
snapped against our clothesline

brush in the pinion jay's nest
lofted of bottle caps, hay strips, and maple twigs

a quiet cavity, space rounded out between
bus seats, their velour fibers like eyelid skin
bunched up beneath this finger tip

Last winter loved no snow
This September, no rain
The vernal stream, no stream

Pines have surrendered their green forever
and blight spots black walnuts and steals their fruit

The barn now craves our hay bales
and the pond depends upon our canoe

Do we obliterate and take away
to make the 10,000 things need us?

Last April, no bees

Our town, no laborers

42nd Street, no hookers

The ocean has no salt and the children sink
with the jellyfish to the bottom

How long will this bus ride drone?
Where did you and the bees go?

For Babylon

From the cages, a roosterish dactyl
followed by two purring churtle-yodels

rip above the din of pet market hawkers
selling their wares and birds to feed their kids

Pretty bird, pretty bird. Good pet, good pet for the girl

From between the bars, the easy song
of the common Iraq babbler

recalls its days hovering in Babylon's ruins
and recovering from the drained Mesopotamian Delta

Pretty song, pretty song. Good song for the ears

From among the crowd a simple woman
with a heavy tongue and ticking heart

explodes into pieces, flesh and feathers splayed together
on the pavilion where there will be no even trade,

no fair exchange today

What Botticelli Could Not See

A woman—cropped silver hair, smart black pants that hug
her heavy hips, dark top that holds her generous breasts,
early 60s—regards Hopper's *A Woman in the Sun* with a
mysterious smirk, pleased perhaps to see a sagging face,
falling but full breasts, wide-eyed pink and purple nipples,
    round yet flabby

buttocks, feet long and bulbous and flat against the floor.
Her weighted eyes stare down the unseen sun, the backdrop
behind her—a rustled bed, tumbled high heels, two black
paintings on walls less blue than sky, an absent
    lover. No golden fleece

flows down her aching back or between her undefined
thighs, no spring flowers drift beside her, no shell floats on
smiling waves beneath fragile feet, no lusty Zephyrs breezes
on her bosoms. Veins and ribs and ankles beneath her flesh,
a rich and fortunate form. All of this the silver-haired

woman gulps in her glance, in her smirk, as she glides past
the painting and strokes her own hips.

A *Raga* for Orpheus

Sukhanusayi Ragah
Attachment comes from pleasure.
   —Patanjali, *Yoga-Sutra-s* II.7

raga (Sanskrit) 1. desire, attachment 2. color, mood 3. considered by
some schools of yoga as one of the chief afflictions or obstacles to
spiritual growth 4. an Indian melodic song played with a season or
time of day

You heard that Orpheus lives down the road
and plays guitar in a blues band trio,
so you caught him last week picking with brio
on silken strings an original, bluesy ode

that wafts the sandy scent of his dead wife,
that vibrates her funny clucking chuckle,
and resurrects her garden of honeysuckle
and mint, the drum of her ceramic knife

against the cutting board. No blame at all
for a backward glance, that reach of the hand
to grasp the quiet way her hands turned

earth with grace: You'll give the god a call
and ask to play the bass in his underground band
and donate a few blues ragas to the urn.

Morning After Rabin's Assassination

Sage maintains its bloom.
No bird song sounds the morning.
Brown magnolia leaves lie scattered

among of still green
grass, boats that cannot hide
in the ravine.

The morning reluctant,
the sun is astonished to find
its hair has turned to gray.

Not to be on Time

Your grandfather kept a car log that dated
his 1968 Riviera's every oil change,

tire rotation, and tune up, a guest book of
promises that if time is mapped

with enough care you will find more of it.
But time shuttles like the steps you and she scooted

across the Hole in the Wall floor to midnight blues,
formless like the lake's lips where you dipped

and found her floating beneath you, beside you like
the wake of wind that blew through that cemetery's

evergreens in Greece where you two glimpsed
someone's father lowered into the ground.

How to let time glide, a day blanketed in the
mountains that rolls without periods

like a sentence written by Faulkner who still
sips brandy and rubs his brow all day,

flesh remade from the pages
of your grandfather's ledgers.

The Artist Works Himself Near-Blind

This morning he heard his eyes fall back into his head
and roll around like his son's marbles in a jar.
Work knocked them out, made pockets of his sockets,
the day's rhythm cut up, no rows to show
what crops he has plowed, only yellow wildflowers growing

in eye holes. A dream dies near dawn
as a blue corpse fades and somewhere near the sink
he hears light appear through the window, pale aqua
light like rays that crawl through the stained glass
chapel windows Matisse designed for his nun friend.

Once the ten thousand things that got his attention—
dust mites pirouetting on the corner of a table
the buzzing timbre of clouds near dawn—
gave the day definition
the way space in a Rothko needs line and color

but his final emotion has clung like a cat to the back
of his head near where his eyes have fallen and blocks
the place where light refracts. Still work
drives him as if penance might come in the next line.

When Picasso asked if Matisse prayed, Matisse said,
No, I meditate. Do you believe in God? Picasso asked.

Yes, when I work.

In a browning photograph a graying Matisse
bed-ridden from age sits up in a bed
and holds a pole, brush tied at the end.
Back to pillow he paints cathedral
walls, a prayer with each stroke. To look

back at day's end and wonder
what marked the way time passed
only small lines drawn on walls tremor,
faint traces of light that quiver
before sleep, answered prayers.

Insomnia

When that light rapping paws the eastern screen
to be let in, I try not to pretend I can count the cats
who fill my dreams or will my way to sleep.
No, I rise like a bubble floating from last night's bath,
drift toward the scruff and itch it in.

My insomnia is princely, prowling,
at once teasing to be stroked
and inching beyond grasp.

"Come here," I whisper, tapping my fingers
on the floor for it to step
within reach. I do not know
what it wants. You can't pin it down
on its back and rub from its belly a genie

to tell me that it comes to resolve last night's fight
because there was no fight, or to goad my fret
about the globe because I know the globe
still swirls in daftness at half past midnight.
Now that I've let it in, I slip outdoors,

walk in the day's flip-side, its briefcase turned inside-out,
papers scattered like stars across the sky, words
as decipherable as the bullfrog's heaving tuba,
and surrender again, this time to the tone of toes
that tick inside the woods and the blood of fear

that like a mosquito has no cause but survival
and to the simple terror and wonder that I
must eventually float out on the water,

flat out on the canoe's floor, and drift
from shore to shore, far away
from the things that purr,

and be awake, stupendously awake in the dark.

3

Move Through

Too much crowds
the house. Pushed out,
something is hidden
or lost. What remains

is not always what you want. Better
select. Cut
away. Slash. Be fierce

as lightning against wood.
What remains:
moonlight lipping cedar
and the voice it recalls.

Woman Burning Another Woman

Aparigrahasthairye janmakathamta sambodah
When a person persists in living without having or wanting excess
possessions, that person will realize the purpose of her birth and the
meaning of life. —Patanjali, Yoga Sutra, II.39

A woman burned by another woman,
you say, bathing me. I try to shake
it away with the soap, ignore the equation
of a bride for a vcr, of burning brides and burning rivers.

We disowned our tv, you remind me, a salve
for being citizen in the land of plastic virtues.
Picture it, you say again.

* * *

She thought she might learn to love her husband,
the one her parents picked for her like a pashmina
shawl on a rack of heirlooms.

> *He blushed*
> *and his new bride laughed and embraced him,*
> *for the knot he had meant to undo*
> *was already untied.*

Words from the *Gatha Saptasati* run
through her like the Ganga's wet tongue,
steady promises milked by her mother's
wishes for a shift in the way men made

oxen of their women. This morning she had woven
a wool blanket for her boy that he might
grow warm, warmer. Her almond eyes wrinkle
in morning's gray light, no trace of her husband.

Her spirit sinks before her in-laws
who, newly arrived, demand from her family
shiny goods as part of the dowry deal—
a tv, new designer jeans, a fast scooter.
They're not kidding.

Her mother-in-law, caught by the fury and furious
no one has delivered her electronic promises,
douses the young woman's hair in oil
and lights a match while the father-in-law
holds the bride down, the boy's blanket

caught in her locks and her hair and dyed
wool swirled together with orange lashes
and her mother-in-law grins at the horrific beauty
that dances across and collapses on
the cold slab floor.

The Stone Goddess's Lament

I emerged a thousand years ago from sand stone,
the handiwork of holy men devout to rhythms
kept by the Arabian Sea and sun and woman.
My form chiseled and framed at my fiercest:
fiery mouth agape, six sword-wielding arms,
riding my lion, sheer force from tools and stone,
image and faith to ward off all their demons.

Each dawn and dusk each bowed to me,
knowing in their bones the revealed stone
would keep order in their precarious world.
Ravi, whose hands first rounded out my form,
the first to see me as I should be seen,
proffered jasmine garlands, heavy with desire,
and slices of mango, the flesh exposed for the taking.

His world has faded. Men come to me now,
nothing in hand except a camera and sneer.
They want a glimpse of secret powers
and a photograph to show their buddies back home.
I'm no goddess but a backdrop to they
who snap my power flash by flash.

The other day three of them arrived,
hands empty. One unfastened his trousers,
the others following in a game to hold
their favorite tool they cannot control
and pissed between my legs,
acid blackening my hips
and eating away at my barren center a hole.

What do men want from us, what do they fear
that they treat us as props and urinals?

A sad sight. When they're not looking,
I will shoot their impressions and zap them.
I will return flat images of themselves
in their lonely dreams and on the walls
of neglected temples they embody,
their dwelling places that one day will erode,
eaten away by their own urine.

Pay Your Rent

Branches of frail mesa bush
hang on an arroyo lip
and spell your due date sideways
to the hard-packed soil.

You try to eavesdrop
but your ears can't hear
below where leaves drop
and a catbird rustles in the lobes.

You lease these ears
to listen to lost languages
but you don't know who
your landlord is.

Listen. Lull your lips
and at last thoughts
will loosen their lasso
around your ears

so feather songs and stone echoes
the syntax of soil
and the spelling of stars
can float in and touch your tongue

and you can pay your rent.

Stories of Cedar

A single log of cedar shaved into
a wooden

ovum canoe slits the waves. Eight rowers born unto

the Northwest Coast water push and
pull, push and

pull the oars whose labor links
the river

to their hands, their sweat, their spirit.
Rowers dream

and conceive the warm womb of their
livelihood

that sustains their rhythm,
chasms from their wake.

* * *

Cedar now lifts finely shaped, lawnless homes above the
water for people who buy aluminum canoes, prefer to rest
above the water where signs shout "No Wakes"

* * *

Somewhere in those lawnless homes some-
one may dwell

who tries to feel Ocean and Moon
making love

underneath her bed, rocking her
soul awake.

Someone's dead myth becomes something
else's lover.

A Mad Man's Grocery List

My grandmother would scan the sky on the way
to the store and ask me to repeat from start to end
her list of words: toothpaste, nuts, eggs. I began,
her slow shadow grounding me but words
from lists wash away by raindrops' forms
dying on my windshield, blurring my sense.

That yolk-haired boy bounded by common sense
is dead. Polysyllabic words now find their way
to my lips–cantaloupe, fettuccine, mortality. The form
of "egg" seemed simple then rounded on each end
something you could hold–not just the word
but the shape that to Brancusi encoded the universe's
     beginning.

Riddled with disease and distraction I begin
the words again on my wife's simple list, sense
my grandmother's heavy hand as she says "Take it one
     word
at a time, slowly, like the clouds," the way
she moved, but words instead end
up scattered along the street's white–striped form.

"Detergent." "Soap." A simple form
that does come from whales whose grandiose shapes begin
to miff me and Ishmael altogether as I try to find an end
to my thoughts along the great white lines, sense
evaporating, liquid planets on the glass exploding the way
I think ~ planets will move closer and a moby word

will help us travel past satellites ~ a guttural word
rising where earth and sky conform
when we will remember each other in a way
with sensus communis, a new beginning
rooting if we direct our sense
away from grocery lists and toward a grander end.

Anyway, who of us will notice the world's old form end?
My grandmother never said a word
about Brancusi but she must have had a sense
for seeing in egg cartons the universe's infant form.
I can't remember the words. Senseless for me to begin
a new list now although new forms appear in my way.

From the parking lot's great white lines I begin to see my
    grandmother's form
etch beside Ishmael to the road's end. He bellows in
    an epic way
as she scans the sky, sensing something about to fall - rain,
    a grand word:

begin, end, sense, form, way, word.

To Attack the Calm

His dog devoured a dove tonight. Among old
pots of basil, the shepherd's grin betrayed
feathers caught between his fangs. He couldn't scold

this beast who's trained for police, taught to raid
the suspicious among us, whose instinctive desire
to roam has been housed and kept and duly caged.

So how could he deny this urge, this dire
need to attack the soft, the domestic, the calm
at night, the urge to leap the fence and fire

away to Mexico, lover in tow, and never look home?
His wife wept and whispered to him to place
on the curb a bag of feathers and small bones:

Then spray the bag with Lysol, dear, to keep the dogs away.
Dogs hunt fear, he thought, and set the tooth-holed
dove on the lawn and whistled for the strays.

The Source

It should suffice for me to say that Rothko's early painting *The Source* contains two forms on a surface, one fourth mainly black, three-fourths off-white over black. One form's shape oblong, a floating pendant perhaps from Costa Rica, or a flat mask from Zaire, scar lines down its nose. The other form, elongated, a shrunken Giacometti form, a charm piece or a bone flute from Peru, texture made by faint brushstrokes, some cheap painter's trick. But my rendering into word-images lies.

I could say one is a flattened gray tick, blood speckled, and the other a painted clothespin or fishing lure: the more domestic, familiar comparisons become bastard boys trying not only to break their way into homes but to replace their impotent fathers. Rothko wanted no facsimiles of more real patterns, reflections in this universe of mirrors, wanted not to play the carnival wizard pulling switches and levers to thrill adolescent viewers in love with themselves, with cheap thrills that recreate nature and ecstasy in the mind. 100 years or so before Rothko, Louise Daguerre's wife called him a lunatic for fixing images in photographs, the mad desire to capture nature in a frame.

So I imagine Rothko, frustrated with nature, closes his eyes more tightly than Cezanne in order to see and to slam the door on the boys who try to enter. Among his estate there are no sketches that resemble DaVinci's of defined male torsos with measured bodies or Vesalius's illustrations of femurs and intestines that appear the year Copernicus completes Revolutions of Celestial Orbs. In the 1950's while Rothko develops a "mature style" scientists amplify light by stimulated emissions of radiation–LASER–image becomes a verb, imaging, to image, some kid scientist says, he among the first generation of scientists whose imaginations have been imprinted by televised projections of Donna Reed or Jackie Gleason, now among the science clan making color maps of brain impulses, the fibers of liver interiors, of June bug wings, the bacteria graphed and colored like tiny roller paint brushes along pen heads and scotch tape strips, the structure of a thunderstorm codified into computer dots & lines,

the song of a mockingbird pinned by color & line according to frequency, pitch, amplitude, tonal pattern, charted and given numbers called "raw data," a sound ascribed a number like a chemical, e.g., gold into Au 79. The frenzy to catalog saps senses. Rothko seemed to sense the danger of trying to render nature, to divide it and place a portion of it into a frame as if our senses and ability to calculate alone could comprehend it. In Boulder last summer I saw retailers selling Lakota tobacco ties for $6, a Ghost Dance dress: $3,800. A totem pole: $850. Bidders at Sotheby's devour their faithless lovers, betrayed by beauty's insistence upon not being whored, vanity, to be re-cataloged and priced. So where, or how, does an artist go?

Manet goes to color patches to distort the eye, while a Hopi woman, face captured in a film documentary, speaks of how she receives patterns of lines in dreams and cannot rest easy until she transforms those patterns in clay, zig-zag, zig-zag, one line responding and referring only to other lines, pure lineage within the bowl's walls curved to hold, the walls themselves receptacles of ornament, function, symbol in one. This rendering, this way of excavating images within is a delicate affair, a fragile trek to uncover a buried relic, an act not of wielding or of measuring as much as receiving and of waiting for the earth's viscera to turn up its innards. The troubled hearts of scientists or men like Conrad's Kurtz forget where the source resides.

Rothko desired to map the heart not like electrocardiograms with graphed PWAVES, QRSWAVES, TWAVES, but with his fingers, with electricity, by listening to the cities throbbing and suffering from hypertension, to resuscitate the alchemical project of van Helmont, to find a way to restore chemical balance through color where forms are weightless, suspended, and gradually, year after year, recognizable comparisons fall away, the media becomes itself.

I cannot imagine now anything that Rothko's forms represent. I imagine only a man whose central organ is not the eye, outward-seeking adventurer that scales the side of a glass building or mountain, but maybe the heart, not for godssake because of its link to Tristan's poisonous potion but because of its persistent pulse, central source that keeps the blood running through veins seen only in open wounds and lined in the whites of our eyes.

A Series of Small Wonders

Three vased twigs of winter berry startle
space that surrounds the farm table,

the ember-hued pellets relished
in her infant pebble pupils

as your matronly arms secure
her dazzle and squirm,

your mouth o'ed by her awe
and the berries astonished by their own glow

Sometimes it is enough to cradle cracks
of light from the wood stove window

and from that tiny opening that quakes
all of it new again and again

4

3 Lagoons

I have travelled through three lagoons
and circled forty-eight moons
and still have not settled down.

Beneath the autumn light caught
in the pond's face
a fish fins by and, curious, knocks on the canoe.

Something is always knocking.
Is this not enough?
If not this, what then?

In the distance a yellow leaf grounds down,
captured in a dusk beam.
Envy of radiant certitude.

The God Spot on Thanksgiving

My mother's friend leans in to say she's mapping
the spot of God in our brains.
We have seizures in the temporal lobe
that release neurochemicals that give us the notion
we live in God's sleeves. *Right there,*

she says pressing her index finger to a spot
on my forehead. *Right there God
might appear or live in your brain.
So you think.*

And there? I ask, finger pointed above
and between her eyebrows, *What lives there?*

She chuckles, *A history of illusions.*

A hummingbird got lost in Central Park
the news anchor reports. No one knows why
but it likely will die soon.

In the backyard near noon a lone gull
several towns from any coast floats
from just above a white-limbed evergreen

as if the tree exhaled it. How to map its path
or the snow's patterns or next week's forecast?
How to track a woman's faith from day to day

and how to measure the wayward dips
the pitch-black days when amnesia dots
awareness like melanoma?

My mother thanks heaven for the twenty inches
of snow that has smothered the mountains in a single day.
The turkey's cooking in the oven.

A day she says to praise and remember.

Her friend laughs again
and the gull vanishes in the snow.

Threat of Apology

       pushes us to the edge
of the kitchen shelf.

We stand there teetering
as if the globe's fate hangs

on your next gesture ~
who will sink a dark name

of another lover into
the other's dawn?

Surprise. You crack and expose
yourself, confess a fault:

Cleopatra cries,
Goddess dies.

But everything regains
another place

as we reassemble
your broken clay pots

that contained your grain, your flour,
your salt.

I savor each piece of you
in my hands

and on my tongue:
bread at communion.

Frida's Throat

Gripped, you iron-waisted lover,
you throttle your country's parrot
and drink its wine
from your husband's hip bones.

Cast away your castanets, darling,
and ride the boar
who rolls up to you
from behind.

Little woman, dark hair above
your lip and below your navel,
lick the sky, scrape its back
with your eyelashes.

You know when your twin
betrays your dream,
when an indigo Chihuahua
discolors your marrow.

A pomegranate sits on
your nightstand, its emerald
teeth lined up like messages
of *muerte*.

You know how to eat it
alone and to share it

too with your lover, your husband,
your father at your next meal.

Don't swallow your own paint.

Speak, woman.
They're waiting,

the thousand girls
who follow you
and the thousand men
who fear you.

Bust the body cast

and squeeze your own breasts
until you make yourself cry,
each tear pigmenting your throat.

No More Silence

No, not silence. This Taoist lives in a hut atop
a Colorado peak these six years
to find subway voices inside a cedar
springs as clear as space in a John Cage piece.
You can venture toward silence any day

but so what, he says. Hu Shih died
at a podium speaking out:
"You cannot write my poems
just as I cannot dream your dreams."

The space of dreams and their borderlands
elude this poet who has been trying to cull
from streams some prisoner's word
that would streak city air with cyanide paint.
Better to be silent than to speak
like a babbling brook. His father's words.

To save their tongues a Chinese poet in the '30s
led an exodus of several hundred students
through central China's mountains
where they warmed themselves
with small fires. Stories, poems
whose language contained the codes
of slave spirituals.

I try to savor silence and not-doing,
I told this Colorado convert.
> *Chestnut tree leaves, now of age,*
> *Complained to the western wind all night long,*
> *Finally win their freedom.*
That was his response, then nothing.

Silence is a luxury and too costly. He said
he was bored with this conversation,
needed to retreat to a dark space
he knew waited in his kitchen

something about the language of spoons
and other objects that muttered of revolutions.
He had words to do, things left unsaid.

A Myth for Your Body

You are secretly blessed when a cat breathes on your arm, it
is written somewhere in a library in Cairo where cats walk
freely through the market squares along the Nile where men
yell out the prices of klipspringer meat and where women
still sell you their straw baskets full of maize and children
will pawn you a palm-sized metal pyramid.

Where cats walk freely along door tops and chair backs,
where your body can't rest, it is written that when a cat
breathes on your arm, ashes of the dragon-slayer
Gilgamesh's former servant fall along your follicles and into
your pores. You are touched. Inside your body a pyramid
slowly is being built by a restless servant without a pharaoh,
without a plan, without Ra, without a vision.

He earnestly assumes the project of your body, someone
else's dwelling. You cannot see him despite your search
each shower or whenever no one's looking. You'd like to
think he plans to build it in the image of some planet to be
discovered a thousand years from now after your bones
have dusted dirt.

Really, you'd just like to know where he's going with all that
fatty tissue, those myriad organs that bellow their own
tunes, one by one those monolithic stones you feel being
hauled in your gut, the ones you refuse to move yourself.

You resolve yourself to blindness and entrust your body to
that humble servant's tiny hands and to the cat who won't
sell you out.

Stand on Turtles

—inspired by an Iroquois tale

The little boy asks what
the earth stands on.

The woman says
it's not what but how

the earth stands
that is the matter. She tries

to speak of a huge mother standing
with her legs spread and someone
else's children gathered underneath,
homeless beneath a bridge, but analogies

falter. Similes flatten. Blueprints overlap.

The woman shrugs, says the earth stands
in the air on a tight wire metaphor.

But how does the metaphor stand?

With care, on another metaphor, she says.
It's metaphors all the way down.

Gathering Fragments of the Davis Mountains

1.
How long has it been
since I have been
with my footsteps?

2.
Space among the oval shells is still

3.
We think we stand atop mountains,
but we sit among thickets

4.
Listen for your name
inscribed in every stone

5.
I am at home for the first Christmas
in years, if not for the very first time

6.
The mountains exhale
the low, lonely damp clouds
and reveal the way home

7.
So much care underground
unfelt by careless eyes

Trunks scar where severed
limbs clear a path

Stones have been thrown
from the road

Clouds have doused the woods,
and words have been carved on stones

You have brought me here
I have brought you here

8.
How do we know
when to leave things alone?

9.
This cave's crevices absorb the Jumano's last cry,
the Comanche's last song,
the wicked wind's and rain's fingerprints,
the laughter and truck ads passing miles away,

and broken pieces of painted glass
held together by a faded label
that reads
ELOB.

Life Sentences and Life Lines

cummings wrote in a not-prose poem that "Life is not a paragraph/And death I think is no parenthesis." But what about the sentence? The same poem claims that "whoever pays attention to the syntax of things/will never wholly kiss you." I'm not so sure. When cummings' mud-puddled days grew numbered, did anyone in any town say the poet with radical measure had broken free from his life sentence?

Did a day for Whitman spread wide and full of contradictions so that by dusk his gulping and galloping body lay sprawled and satiated, drunk with soldier hats and oak trees and muscular arms, his voice all rasp and cedar as he rambled a deviant lover and himself to sleep beneath the stars?

Did a day for Dickinson / measure itself / with buzz and flash / —noon a iamb / and dusk a dash?

Did Baudelaire, free of line breaks and measured feet, write in ways that let his days assume a form built by the marching madness of the unbroken line, Monday slouching into Tuesday and Tuesday sneaking into March, the intoxicated faith that the simple and unbidden act of lining up word after wine itself would shuttle him across night on a bat wing?

On a white beach peppered with black pebbles shaped like letters Ponge waves a day that will by dark round out and burn bright like a toked cigarette ash if only for a second or two, cleaving each word to prolong the end.

What is a life sentence without line breaks? The days grow brambles. Telephone poles tooth picked over pines become lighthouses—no, pillars of tight wires laid out like lines to follow to Poetry, Texas. And when the Man gets there, the diner disappoints not with its metallic fried food but because it hides no metaphors in the corner where a girl, maybe 17, broods in a booth and reads a worn copy of *Tropics of Capricorn*. She will not lead him out of the diner. She is a dead end.

And that's what we do, isn't it? Keep fending off the end of the sentence perhaps to find a space, an opening, to break free?

Tanning Desire

When her arm brushed against mine
tonight while washing rice grains
down the drain, I wished to stain

her grin in relief by a kitchen light bulb,
the first soft connection in a year.

To tan memories I've felled a hemlock
paper forest, bundles of bark gathered
to harden a fleeting image into a belt or boots,
something endurable and wearable.
But what stays in this saddled mind?

When we two stole away to a cabin,
the open flesh of the pomegranate
she proffered me once as a truce—
that pickled desire my hands hold still,

stained palms silhouetted on paper.

Countdown

This one young red-tailed hawk scissors
this singular gray April air
above this still-barren willow
on this late still-birthed morning.

One piping plover at a time, one
small brown bat at a time, one
European honey bee at a time, wings

vanish.

One mustard seed at a time,
one feverfew stem at a time, one
banana leaf at a time, foods

vanish.

One milkweed cheek at a time, one
shagbark trunk at a time, one
corpulent torso at a time, textures

vanish.

One Teut-Tang drum dance at a time, one
hootenanny at a time, one
Inuit kunik at a time, gestures

vanish.

One holy tongue at a time, one
cradle song at a time, one
Gregorian chant at a time, one
child's prayer at a time, voices

vanish

and the ten thousand things
become nine thousand, become eight
thousand
seven
six
five
four three two

one.

Hold on, young hawk,
for this one morning,
hold on for this singular kind of one.

Heron

weightless stone with wings
here on water

here
on the brink of day
as sky's third eye winks
at you behind orange clouds

in the wish of dawn
in the whish of water
find a fish that calls you

and take in your beak
and down your long throat
these aches of needy company
these tugs from insistent voices

and lift me with you
weightless limb with wings
that we may blend in among the willow
and early light the hue of blue sibilants
steady and still

here on the limb
our wings and head fold in
our form a long closed eyelid
the quiet confidence of being alone
waves in our wake

here in pale light
here on water
here on air
heron

ACKNOWLEDGEMENTS

The author gratefully acknowledges the editors of the following magazines and journals that have published these poems:

> The Comstock Review–"To Attack the Calm"
> Concho River Review–"Gathering Fragments of the Davis Mountains"
> New York Spirit–"The Stone Goddess's Lament"
> Oberon–"Woman Burning Another Woman"
> Sentence: A Journal of Prose Poetics–"The Source," "Life Lines and Sentences"

I am grateful to Melissa Studdard for her careful review of this manuscript and for encouraging me to listen to the manuscript's structural music. Thank you to Philip Pardi who in his thoughtful review of the manuscript was able to place the poems within the tradition of poets I hope it is aligned with. Gratitude to Will Nixon for his friendship and for his word-by-word reading in which he gently called out certain poems' weaknesses and pointed me toward their strengths.

ABOUT THE AUTHOR

JEFFREY DAVIS is a writer, speaker, and consultant. He is author of the nonfiction book *The Journey from the Center to the Page: Yoga Philosophies and Practices As Muse for Authentic Writing* (Penguin 2004; Monkfish Publishing, 2008) and the poetry collections *City Reservoir* (BarnBurner Press 2000) and *Coat Thief* (Saint Julian Press 2016).

HE has received fellowships from the Virginia Center for the Creative Arts and Woodstock's Byrdcliffe Artist's Colony and has served for several years as fiction editor for *Tiferet Journal*. He has taught most recently at Western Connecticut State University's MFA in Professional & Creative Writing Program as well as at leading centers & conferences around the world.

HE writes an online column on the science of creativity for Psychology Today and for The Creativity Post and also heads up the renegade team at Tracking Wonder Consultancy. He lives with his wife and their two girls in a farmhouse in New York's Hudson Valley.

LEARN more at: http://trackingwonder.com

Book Interior Design
Front Matter - Perpetua Titling MT and Garamond Font
Poem Titles – Garamond 14 Point Font
Poems – Garamond 11.5 Point Font

CPSIA information can be obtained at www.ICGtesting.com
Printed in the USA
LVOW10s1729120516

487960LV00002B/292/P